THE ECONOMY of God AND THE BUILDING UP OF THE BODY OF CHRIST

WITNESS LEE

Living Stream Ministry
Anaheim, California • www.lsm.org

© 1989 Living Stream Ministry

All rights reserved. No part of this work may be reproduced or transmitted in any form or by any means—graphic, electronic, or mechanical, including photocopying, recording, or information storage and retrieval systems—without written permission from the publisher.

First Edition, May 1989.

ISBN 978-0-87083-441-7 (hardcover)
ISBN 978-0-87083-442-4 (softcover)

Published by

Living Stream Ministry
2431 W. La Palma Ave., Anaheim, CA 92801 U.S.A.
P. O. Box 2121, Anaheim, CA 92814 U.S.A.

Printed in the United States of America

12 13 14 15 16 17 / 12 11 10 9 8 7 6 5

CONTENTS

Title	Page
Preface	5
1 A View of God's Economy from the Old Testament Types (1)	7
2 A View of God's Economy from the Old Testament Types (2)	19
3 A View of God's Economy from the New Testament Revelation (1)	33
4 A View of God's Economy from the New Testament Revelation (2)	43
5 The Building Up of the Body of Christ (1)	53
6 The Building Up of the Body of Christ (2)	63

PREFACE

This small book is composed of messages translated from Chinese of a conference given by Brother Witness Lee in Seoul, Korea during November 5 to 8, 1988.

CHAPTER ONE

A VIEW OF GOD'S ECONOMY
FROM THE OLD TESTAMENT TYPES

(1)

Scripture Reading: Col. 2:17; Heb. 8:5; 10:1a

OUTLINE

I. Individual types:
  A. Adam and Eve—Christ and the church—Gen. 2:18, 21-24; Eph. 5:30-32:
    1. Adam—Christ as the expression of God.
    2. Eve—the church as the expression of Christ.
  B. From Adam, the fallen one, to Noah, the one who worked together with God—from a fallen sinner to a saint working together with the Lord:
    1. The fallen Adam wearing the skin of the sacrifice—a sinner receiving Christ as his covering righteousness—Gen. 3:21; Gal. 3:27; 1 Cor. 1:30.
    2. Abel, the one inheriting salvation, offering up a lamb as a sacrifice—a believer living in Christ to become the righteousness of God, being acceptable to Him—Gen. 4:4; 2 Cor. 5:21.
    3. Enosh, the frail one, calling on the name of Jehovah—a frail believer calling on the name of the Lord to enjoy Him as his portion—Gen. 4:26; Acts 9:14; 2 Tim. 2:22; 1 Cor. 1:2.
    4. Enoch, the one pursuing after God, walking with God—a believer who pursues after the Lord living together with the Lord—Gen. 5:22-24; John 14:19b; Gal. 2:20.
    5. Noah, the one walking with God, working with Him—a believer who lives together with the

Lord working together with the Lord to work out his own salvation—Gen. 6:9b, 14, 18; Phil. 2:12b.

C. Abraham, Isaac, and Jacob with Joseph—the threefold experience of a called believer in the Triune God, from his selection to his reigning:
1. As the father, Abraham being called by God and justified by faith, living by faith and living in fellowship with God—a believer experiencing the calling and justification of God the Father, by faith living a life of fellowshipping with Him—Gen. 12:1; 15:6; Heb. 11:9; Gen. 18:1, 17, 22-33; 1 Cor. 1:9; Rom. 8:30; Gal. 2:20b; 1 John 1:3, 6.
2. As the son, Isaac by faith inheriting all the promised blessings—a believer living in fellowship with God experiencing the inheritance of all the grace in God the Son for the enjoyment in satisfaction and rest—Gen. 25:5; Heb. 11:9; Eph. 3:6; Gal. 3:29.
3. As the one inheriting from his grandfather and his father, Jacob being chosen by God, experiencing trials to become the Israel of God, bringing God's blessing to everyone—a believer chosen by God, enjoying the love of God the Father and the grace of God the Son, experiencing the transformation of God the Spirit through trials in his environment, to become a mature man to bestow God's blessings upon others—Gen. 25:23; Rom. 9:10-13; Gen. 27:41-45; 31:1-2; 32:28; 47:7, 10; 48:9, 15-16, 20; 49:26, 28; 1 Pet. 1:2; Rom. 8:28; 2 Cor. 3:18; 1 Cor. 15:58; Heb. 6:1; Rom. 12:14.
4. As the one who in experience forms a part of Jacob, Joseph reigning and dispensing widely the riches of God to everyone—a believer who is transformed, overcoming, and mature, reigning for the Lord and dispensing the riches of God in Christ to everyone—Gen. 41:40-44, 55-57; 2 Cor. 2:14-16; Eph. 3:8; Rev. 20:4, 6.

Prayer: Lord, our hearts are rejoicing, and our spirits are praising. You are the Lord of grace. We look to You for the meeting tonight. May You visit every one of us. We praise You that whenever You gather us together into Your name, You speak to us and give grace to us. Speak to us again tonight, and be gracious to us again. May everyone receive the portion reserved for him, and may everyone touch You and gain You. May You speak in our speaking and visit every one of us in our speaking. May You even glorify Your own name and bind Your enemy, Satan. Lord, for the sake of Your testimony, Your church, and Your recovery in Korea today, grant us Your blessing in many ways that You may gain the ground and have Your way in this land that this whole nation would be blessed. In Your mighty name we pray. Amen.

In this conference we have received the burden from the Lord to consider the matter of God's economy. The word economy in Greek means house law. It refers to the household management or household administration and is understood to mean an administrative arrangement, a plan, an intention, or a proposal. From this wonderful term we can see that the God we believe in and whom we serve is a God of purpose, plan, move, and activity. He is full of matters related to His economy. Even before the foundation of the earth, He in Christ made a plan and a decision, that is, an arrangement and a proposal. Hence, He has set forth an economy for the ages.

Superficially, it seems the Old Testament is a record of stories of individuals, a history of the nation of Israel, plus some songs, proverbs, and prophecies. Although you cannot find the word economy there, yet God's economy is there. When we come to the New Testament, especially when we come to the Epistles of the Apostle Paul, the one who received the highest and the greatest revelation, we find that he repeatedly used the term economy. In Ephesians 1 he said that God, according to His good pleasure, has an economy for the ages, which is to head up all things in Christ (vv. 9-10). In chapter three he told us again that God is accomplishing this through the church. The church is the highest means whereby God heads up all things under the authority of

Christ for the fulfillment of His economy (vv. 9-10). The entire book of Ephesians shows us how God accomplishes His economy through the church by the Triune God working Himself into tripartite men whom He created so that He could be their life, life element, and life sphere to constitute them the church. Through the church, God will head up all things in Christ. By the time we come to 1 Timothy 1, we see Paul telling his co-worker Timothy to remain in Ephesus to charge people not to teach things other than God's economy (vv. 3-4). This shows us that any doctrine that causes the saints to deviate from the central lane and ultimate goal of God's economy is a different teaching and is a deception of Satan. We need to emphasize God's economy again and again, so that it becomes the central lane and ultimate goal for our Christian life.

THE BASIC THOUGHT CONCERNING GOD'S ECONOMY

Our God is a unique God. He is the Lord of all creation. For His economy, however, there is a distinction of three. He is the Father, the Son, and the Spirit. The Father, the Son, and the Spirit are the three Persons, or three hypostases of the one God. The Father is the source, the Son is the expression, and the Spirit is the entering in. In eternity past, He was the Father, hidden in light, unapproachable by man, being invisible and untouchable. One day, in time, He put on human flesh and came among men, manifesting Himself visibly before men. This is the Son, who was called Jesus. When He came, He did not come by Himself, leaving the Father behind. Rather, He came from the Father and with the Father. While He was living and moving on earth, the Holy Father was with Him, and the Holy Spirit was leading Him in everything. Hence, the whole Triune God was in Jesus. When man sees Jesus he sees the Son, and he who has the Son has the Father, and he who has the Father has the Spirit. This shows us that the Father is the source and that the Son is the expression. Then the Son went to the cross to die there. After that He entered into resurrection, and the Spirit was manifested. Therefore, the Spirit is the realization of the Son and is also the entering in of the Son. This Spirit enters into all those who believe in the Lord and becomes their life, their life supply, and their everything. In this way, the Triune God is joined to man and even mingles with man. This is the story on God's side. Our God is triune.

On man's side, we are also of three parts. Outwardly we have a body. Inside the body we have the soul. Within the soul is the spirit. Hence, Paul said in 1 Thessalonians that God wants to sanctify our whole spirit, soul, and body (5:23). Although we are small, we are not simple. Within this small man, there are a lot of levels. Outwardly we have a visible form. Within this form there is a soul, which is our personality, the seat of our self. In the depth of our being, there is still one more part, which is our spirit. The spirit is for us to worship God and to contact God. If we exercise our mind, we will not find God. But if we would forget our thoughts and would exercise our spirit to call "O Lord Jesus" a few times, we will touch God in the depth of our being and will feel that God has touched us. This proves that our spirit within us wants God. It also proves that God is real, true, and living. If you call any other name such as that of Confucius or Washington, you will not have any feeling, even if you were to call a hundred times. The reason for this is that they are all dead and buried. But if you call "O Lord Jesus" in whatever language, whether it be English, Korean, or Chinese, you will have a certain feeling within. Perhaps you will feel that you have wronged Him. Perhaps you will want to praise Him, or perhaps you will want to tell others how good Jesus is. This proves that Jesus is the living God, and He is living within you. I believe all of us who have believed in the Lord Jesus have this kind of experience.

Hence, we have to see that the God revealed in the Bible is the Triune God. He is the Father, the Son, and the Spirit. We also are of three parts. The Triune God desires to work Himself into the tripartite man. First, He enters into our spirit to regenerate us. Next, He wants to increase His territory within us. He desires to expand from our spirit to our mind, emotion, and will. This requires that we hand ourselves completely over to Him. We have to surrender to Him our mind, thoughts, emotion, love, and decisions. In this matter we always have our reservations, and we are always debating and bargaining with the Lord. The Lord is not satisfied with gaining our spirit only. He wants to go one step further to gain our soul.

What is sanctification? To be sanctified is to have the Lord Jesus gain our inward parts step by step. When the Lord gains your mind, your mind is sanctified. When He gains your emotion, your emotion is sanctified. This is the renewing and transforming mentioned in the New Testament. Our spirit is sanctified already, but our soul must be transformed. Now the Lord is transforming us every day until the day He comes when He will transfigure our body. By then even our body will be sanctified, and He will gain all of the tripartite man. Our spirit, soul, and body will all be occupied and saturated by Him, and He will be fully manifested from within us. This is the basic thought of God's economy.

God's economy is the Triune God working Himself bit by bit into us the tripartite men. The revelation of the New Testament shows us that the Lord Jesus who saved us is the embodiment of the Triune God. He desires to work the Triune God—the Father, the Son, and the Spirit—into us. Therefore, we the believers have the Father in us, the Son in us, and the Spirit in us. Paul said in 2 Corinthians 13:14, "The grace of the Lord Jesus Christ, and the love of God, and the fellowship of the Holy Spirit be with you all." The Triune God—the Father, the Son, and the Spirit—is enjoyed by us here. How mysterious! Our God is not one but three. But though He is three, yet He is still one. Our human mind can never understand this. We can only acknowledge it as such. The entire Triune God is here; the love of the Father is here, the grace of the Son is here, and the fellowship of the Spirit is also here.

This is not all. On our side, we are not of one part only. Rather, we are of three parts. There is the spirit, the soul, and the body. The Triune God is not just in our spirit; He is spreading out from our spirit. The question is whether or not we would allow Him to spread. Are we willing to be subject to Him and to give Him all the ground? When we give Him all the ground, He will gain us completely to be His living members, coordinating with all the members to become His Body. This is God's economy. The whole Bible is a record of this. In the Old Testament it is revealed in types. In the New Testament it is unfolded in revelation.

INDIVIDUAL TYPES

In this chapter we will first look at God's economy in the types of the Old Testament. If we read the Old Testament carefully, we will see that it is roughly divided into two sections. The first section is a history of nine persons. The second section is a history of the nation of Israel. Both the history of the nine persons and the history of the nation of Israel are types and pictures. They both describe the same thing—God's economy.

We will first consider the first section of the Old Testament which is the story of nine persons recorded in the fifty chapters of the book of Genesis. The first five persons of these nine form one group—Adam, Abel, Enosh, Enoch, and Noah. The last four form another group—Abraham, Isaac, Jacob, and Joseph. The first group shows us how God works Himself into the sinner. The last group shows us how this man into whom God has worked Himself experiences Him as the Father, the Son, and the Spirit. In the end the sinner becomes Israel, who is the prince of God, ruling for God and dispensing His riches into men.

ADAM AND EVE—CHRIST AND THE CHURCH

Adam—Christ as the Expression of God

Among these nine persons, the first is Adam and Eve. Adam is a type in two aspects. After his creation and before his fall, he was a type of Christ who is the embodiment of God. Adam was created by God according to His own image for the purpose of expressing Him. God also entrusted him with the authority to rule over all things to represent Him. Hence the created Adam is a type of Christ expressing God and ruling for God as the Head.

Eve—the Church as the Expression of Christ

God took a rib from Adam to form a woman (Gen. 2:22) who is Eve, his wife. Eve is a type of the church as the expression of Christ. As Eve was from Adam, so the church is from Christ. [This picture shows us the desire of God in His economy.] God is the unique Male in the universe. He needs a counterpart (Gen. 2:18) which is the created man, redeemed and regenerated by Christ, transformed, and built together to become the church. This is why at the end of the Bible we see the Spirit and the bride speaking as one man in Revelation 22:17. The Spirit is the ultimate expression of the Triune God. He is the processed Triune God. He has a bride which means that He is married to the created, redeemed, regenerated, transformed, and glorified tripartite man. This matter was mentioned by John the Baptist in John 3: "He who has the bride is the bridegroom" (v. 29). The Bridegroom is the Lord Jesus, and the bride is the church. Ephesians 5 also says that as Adam and Eve were made husband and wife, so Christ and the church are made one body (vv. 30-32). When we come to Revelation 19, we see that the marriage of the Lamb is come (v. 7). Chapter twenty-one says that the holy city, New Jerusalem, comes down out of heaven from God, prepared as a bride adorned for her husband (v. 2). The New Jerusalem is on the one hand the dwelling place of God, and on the other hand the bride of the Lamb. The Lamb is the embodiment of the Triune God, and the Lamb's bride is a composition of the redeemed ones throughout the ages. [In eternity future the Triune God will become one body with His redeemed tripartite man. The two will become one universal couple. This is the goal of God's economy.]

FROM ADAM, THE FALLEN ONE, TO NOAH, THE ONE WHO WORKED TOGETHER WITH GOD

Not long after Adam was created, he fell and became the first sinner. He is, therefore, a type of the sinner. On the side of creation, he represents Christ. On the side of the fall, he represents us the sinners. From Adam, the fallen one, to Noah, the one working together with God, we have a type of the fallen sinner becoming a saint working together with God. We were all Adam, fallen sinners. But God has saved us and has made us step by step to be Noah, working together with God and building an ark for Him.

The Fallen Adam Wearing
the Skin of the Sacrifice

When Adam sinned, he knew that he was naked and had nowhere to hide himself (Gen. 3:7-8). God gave him the skin of the sacrifice for coats (3:21) to be his covering. This typifies that we, the descendants of Adam and the fallen sinners, are all naked and are not able to stand before God. But the Lord Jesus has become the Lamb of God (John 1:29) having been slain for us and having shed His blood to redeem us from our sins. Moreover, He gave Himself to us to be our righteous covering. Hence, we who have believed and are baptized into Christ have put on Christ (Gal. 3:27) and are able to stand before God.

Abel, the One Inheriting Salvation,
Offering Up a Lamb as a Sacrifice

After Adam we have Abel. Genesis 4:4 says that Abel offered up a lamb as a sacrifice for God's acceptance. This typifies that we, the saved ones who have put on Christ, live daily in Christ to live Him out, that we would become the righteousness of God (2 Cor. 5:21). When we offer up this Christ that we live out as a sacrifice to God for His satisfaction, we are accepted by God in Him.

Enosh, the Frail One,
Calling On the Name of Jehovah

The third person is Enosh. The meaning of his name is the frail one. He called on the name of Jehovah. This is a type of the frail believer calling on the name of the Lord to enjoy Him as his portion. After we are saved, we put on Christ as our righteousness before God and learn to live in Him to live Him out. But many times we feel that we are weak and not able to overcome our own weaknesses. The only way is to call "O Lord Jesus!" By calling on His name, we overcome to enjoy the riches of the Lord.

Enoch, the One Pursuing after God, Walking with God

The fourth person is Enoch, the one pursuing after God and walking with God. He is a type of the believer who pursues after the Lord and who lives and moves together with the Lord. When you are about to lose your temper or show a long face, you can experience victory, walk with the Lord, and live together with Him by calling on the name of the Lord. In this way you are changed from an "Enosh" to an "Enoch," from a weak believer to one who walks with the Lord.

Noah, the One Walking with God, Working with Him

The fifth person is Noah. Noah worked with God to build the ark. This is one step further from Enoch's walking with God. First, the fallen sinner Adam puts on Christ, being acceptable to God to become Abel. Then through his weakness, he becomes Enosh who calls on the Lord all the time. As a further step, he becomes Enoch who walks with God. As a result, he becomes Noah who works together with God, building the ark every day, not only for the salvation of others, but to save himself as well. Philippians 2:12 says to "work out your own salvation with fear and trembling." Today we all have to be in fear and trembling, walking with God, working together with Him to build our own ark, so that we can save not only others but also ourselves from the judgment of God and the corrupted age into a new age. In this new age, we live before God to offer up the burnt offering for God's satisfaction.

Adam, Abel, Enosh, Enoch, and Noah form the first group of five people. Their history is a picture of every believer. We are sinners saved by God to the extent that we become those who work together with God.

ABRAHAM, ISAAC, AND JACOB WITH JOSEPH

After Noah, there are four more persons—Abraham, Isaac, and Jacob with Joseph. They form one group. They typify the called believer's threefold experience of the Triune God from his selection to his reigning.

As the Father, Abraham Being Called by God and Justified by Faith, Living by Faith and Living in Fellowship with God

If we have the experience of the first group of five people, we will surely experience God the Father in the way of Abraham's experience. Abraham was one called by God and justified by faith, who lived by faith and lived in fellowship with God. This is a type of the believer experiencing the calling and justification of God the Father and by faith living a life of fellowshipping with Him. Our experience of the Triune God is similar to that experienced by Abraham. God the Father first called us. Then we walk by Him, living by faith and living in fellowship with Him.

As the Son, Isaac by Faith Inheriting All the Promised Blessings

After we have the experience of Abraham, we enjoy all the riches of the Father deposited in the Son. This is the experience of Isaac. Isaac by faith inherited all the promised blessings. This is a type of a believer who lives in fellowship with God experiencing the inheritance of all the grace in God the Son for the enjoyment in satisfaction and rest. Abraham left everything to Isaac. We who belong to Christ are the descendants of Abraham. We also have inherited an inheritance according to the promise for the enjoyment in satisfaction and rest.

As the One Inheriting from His Grandfather and His Father, Jacob Being Chosen by God Experiencing Trials to Become the Israel of God, Bringing God's Blessing to Everyone

After we experience the riches of the Son, God the Spirit will lead us to experience Jacob's portion. Jacob was chosen by God to experience trials to become the Israel of God, bringing God's blessing to everyone. This is a type of the believer chosen by God who enjoys the love of God the Father and the grace of God the Son and experiences the transformation of

God the Spirit through trials in his environment to become a mature man to bestow God's blessings to others. When we who are in Christ enjoy His riches, the Spirit will lead us to pass through all kinds of trials in our environment to be transformed by the Spirit to become Israel, the prince of God.

As the One Who in Experience Forms a Part of Jacob, Joseph Reigning and Dispensing Widely the Riches of God to Everyone

Joseph in experience forms a part of Jacob. He reigned in Egypt for God, dispensing all the rich food to the whole world. This is a type of the transformed, overcoming, and mature believer reigning for the Lord, dispensing the riches of God in Christ to everyone.

Hence, from the experience of the first group of five people, we go on to experience the Father, the Son, and the Spirit. In the end, we all become Israel, the prince of God, reigning for God and dispensing the riches of God in Christ to everyone. This is what the second group of four people typifies. The experiences of these nine people tell us how God accomplishes His economy in us, the believers. Today, although every one of us is different in our spiritual experience—some being higher, while others are lower—we have to look to God's mercy that we would go on and advance further and further in the process of God's economy.

A message given by Brother Witness Lee in Seoul, Korea on November 5, 1988.

CHAPTER TWO

A VIEW OF GOD'S ECONOMY FROM THE OLD TESTAMENT TYPES

(2)

Scripture Reading: Col. 2:17; Heb. 8:5; 10:1a

OUTLINE

II. The corporate type:
  A. The corporate Israel—the church as the Body of Christ—Exo. 12:3a; Gal. 1:2; 6:16:
    1. Experiencing the Passover, having God's judgment pass over them—the whole church experiencing Christ as the Passover—Exo. 12:21, 13; 1 Cor. 5:7-8.
    2. Leaving Egypt and crossing the Red Sea—the believers baptized to be delivered from the world—Exo. 12:41; 14:22, 29-30; 1 Cor. 10:1-2; 1 Pet. 3:21.
    3. Passing through the wilderness to offer sacrifices to God—the believers being led by God to serve God—Exo. 3:18; Matt. 28:19-20.
    4. Experiencing the bitter water turned sweet—the believers experiencing the bitter situation turned sweet through the cross—Exo. 15:23-25; 2 Cor. 6:9-10.
    5. Enjoying the manna from heaven as the daily supply—the believers enjoying Christ as their daily life supply—Exo. 16:14-15, 31; 1 Cor. 10:3; John 6:48-51, 57b.
    6. Drinking the living water which flowed from

the rock—the believers drinking of Christ as the living water—Exo. 17:6; 1 Cor. 10:4; John 7:37-39; 1 Cor. 12:13.
7. Defeating Amalek—the believers overcoming the flesh by the Holy Spirit—Exo. 17:8-16; Gal. 5:16-17.
8. Coming to the mountain appointed by God, receiving revelation, and erecting the tabernacle—the believers being led by the Lord to receive revelation and build the church as God's dwelling place—Exo. 19:1-6; 25:8-9; Eph. 2:18-22.
9. Wandering and dying in the wilderness—the believers wandering and failing in the soul—Num. 14:32-33; Heb. 3:12-13; 4:1, 11-12.
10. Crossing the river Jordan and entering into Canaan, the good land—the believers' natural life passing through the death of Christ and in resurrection their enjoying Christ as the good land—Josh. 3:14-17; 4:8-9; Col. 3:1-4; 1:12.
11. Defeating the enemy, gaining the land, and building the temple—the believers defeating the spiritual enemies, gaining the territory in Christ, and building up the church as God's temple—1 Chron. 22:17-18; Eph. 6:10-20; 2:21-22.
12. Becoming desolate, failing, and being carried away to Babylon—the church becoming desolate, failing, and being carried away to the mysterious Great Babylon—2 Chron. 36:11-20; Rev. 2:14-15, 20; 17:5.
13. Returning from captivity to Jerusalem to rebuild the temple of God on the original foundation—being recovered from the Great Babylon to the original ground of the church to rebuild the church of God—Ezra 1:1-11; 3:3-13; Rev. 3:1, 4, 7-12; 18:4.
14. Rebuilding the city of Jerusalem as the circumference of God's temple, and further rebuilding

the temple and the city of Jerusalem during the coming restoration of the nation of Israel—the overcomers in the church and the overcoming saints of the Old Testament eventually becoming the New Jerusalem in the millennium, ultimately consummating in the New Jerusalem in the new heaven and the new earth to be the enlargement of God's temple—Neh. 2:17-18; Ezek. 40:2, 5; 48:15-16, 30-35; Rev. 3:12; 21:1-2.
B. The entire tabernacle and the temple having the ark as the center—the church being the enlargement of Christ with Christ as the center—Exo. 40:2-3; 1 Kings 7:51; 8:1-6; Col. 3:10-11.

Prayer: Lord, by Your precious blood we look to You again. You are the Lord who is with us and the One who speaks to us. This morning reveal Yourself to us through Your word. Speak to each one of us, and touch the spirit of every one of us that everyone would feel Your presence in the Spirit and would feel deeply that You are near us and are being gracious to us. Lord, open up Your word. Shine forth the light from Your word and enlighten us. Vindicate that You are one spirit with us and that we are one spirit with You. May our spirit be joined to Your Spirit, and may Your Spirit be mingled with our spirit. Lord, send down Your blessing and pour it out upon everyone who is here in this meeting. Cover us also with Your victorious blood. Oppose the power of darkness for us. Bind Your enemy who is also our enemy. By Your victorious name we pray. Amen.

We have seen that in eternity past, before the creation of all things, God had an eternal economy which is simply to dispense the Triune God Himself into the tripartite man. On God's side, He is triune, with the Father, the Son, and the Spirit. On man's side, we are tripartite, with a spirit, a soul, and a body. The God who lives in unapproachable light is the Father; He is the source. When He is manifested, He is the Son. When He visits us, cares for us, and comes upon us, He is the Spirit. This Spirit enters into our spirit to be mingled with our spirit. In this way the two spirits become one spirit. Hence, the spirit is the highest part of man. If you live in the spirit, you are the most uplifted person, one of the highest class. If you live in the soul, you are much lower; you are of the second class. If you live in the body, you are the lowest of all; you are of the third class. For this reason, do not remain in the soul or the body. Rather, you should strive to get into the spirit to touch the Spirit of God and to be mingled with Him.

When the Triune God—the Father, the Son, and the Spirit—enters into the spirit, the soul, and the body, man becomes one with God. This is what God in His economy has purposed to accomplish. This matter is recorded in the Bible in a plain and clear way. Unfortunately, when most people read the Bible, they see only the stories on the surface; they do not see the revelation in its depths. They see only that Adam ate of the forbidden fruit and committed a mortal sin, that Abel offered a sacrifice acceptable to God, that Enosh called on the name of Jehovah, etc. They do not see much significance in these things. Actually, all these things are recorded in the Bible as types. They are there to show us how God accomplishes His economy. When Adam sinned and fell, he hid himself and dared not see God's face. God came to seek him out and covered him with coats of skin from the sacrifice. Surely he must have been full of gratitude to God, and God's Spirit surely must have entered into him then. The issue was Abel. Abel offered sacrifices to God, thereby having a further contact with God, resulting in God's Spirit entering into him. Then we come to Enosh who called on the name of Jehovah in his weakness, and the Spirit of God again entered into him. Following that, Enoch walked with God. It must have been due to God's working Himself into Enoch and joining Himself to his spirit that he was able to walk with God. After Enoch there was Noah. Not only did Noah walk with God, but he also worked together with God to build the ark. This also must have been done through God's Spirit contacting and fellowshipping with man's spirit.

This matter is proved by Genesis 6:3. There it says that the Spirit of Jehovah would no longer abide in man forever, for he had become flesh (see margin ASV). We see from this that from Genesis 1 to Genesis 5, from Adam to Noah, the Spirit of Jehovah was abiding with man. It was due to the fact that the Spirit of Jehovah was abiding in him that the fallen and sinful Adam was able to obtain God's redemption. In the same way, it was due to the fact that the Spirit of Jehovah was with Abel that he offered sacrifice to God. That Enosh would call on the name of Jehovah, that Enoch would walk with God, and that Noah would work with God were all due to the fact that the Spirit of Jehovah was with them.

Today when we call "O Lord Jesus," it is also due to the fact that the Holy Spirit is with us. First Corinthians 12:3 says, "No one can say, Lord Jesus, except in the Holy Spirit." When we call on the Lord Jesus, it proves that the Holy Spirit is with us. The presence of the Holy Spirit is the coming of the Triune God into us. First, He enters into our spirit. Then He spreads to our soul, uplifting and transforming it. Finally, He will uplift our body, transfiguring it into a glorious body like His own. Hence, God's coming to save us is a gradual descent, working Himself into us to effect in us a gradual ascent. First He enters into our spirit, then He uplifts our soul, and then He uplifts our body that we may become the same as He is. Before we were saved, all day long our thoughts, desires, and decisions were on low and dishonorable things. After we are saved, the Spirit of God enters into us to uplift our soul. Now the things we think, desire, and decide in our heart are much higher than before. Moreover, they are daily being uplifted higher and higher. Not only is our soul uplifted; even the functions of our body are uplifted. Before we were saved, our mouth frequently spoke evil words, and our feet walked the way of corruption. Now our mouth speaks words of praise, words of the gospel, and words that build others up. Our feet are now walking to the place of the church meeting. Today we are no longer the fallen Adam; we are Noah. We have been uplifted by the Triune God. We are all high-class people. On the one hand, we offer sacrifices to God and call on His name. On the other hand, we walk with God and work with God. This is what God has planned and intended. It is what He wants to obtain in His economy.

This is not all. When we go on further, we will realize that all that we pass through is the experience of the love of the Father, the grace of the Son, and the fellowship of the Spirit. In our experience, there is a part which is what Abraham experienced. There is also a part which is what Isaac experienced, and there is a part which is what Jacob experienced. Jacob was a supplanter. Even while he was in his mother's womb, he took hold of his brother Esau's heel (Gen. 25:26). When he grew up, he cheated to take Esau's blessing from his father (27:23). After he escaped to the house of Laban his uncle, he still used deceiving means to turn the flock into his own (30:42). But he could not escape the transforming hand of God. In the end, the transforming work of the Holy Spirit totally transformed him. When he was old and mature in life, not only did he no longer deceive others, but his supplanting hands were turned into blessing hands, blessing people everywhere. When he went to Egypt and saw Pharaoh, he blessed Pharaoh (47:10). He also blessed the two sons of Joseph, Ephraim and Manasseh (48:9). Before he died, he gave a separate blessing to each of his twelve sons (49:28). The supplanting Jacob became Israel, the prince of God. Joseph came out of Jacob. He represented the reigning aspect of Jacob. He was commissioned by Pharaoh to rule over the whole land of Egypt (41:43). At the time when famine was over the whole world, he distributed the rich food to all the people. All these are works in God's economy.

Hence, the experiences of all these nine persons in Genesis are part of God's economy. God worked Himself into every one of them and worked every one of them into Him. They were joined and mingled with God and were transformed, even to become the prince of God, reigning for God on earth and distributing to others His riches. This experience was high enough. But it was only on the individual side. God had not yet obtained a corporate dwelling place. He still did not have a place on earth in which to dwell.

THE CORPORATE TYPE

The Corporate Israel

God's intention is to have a corporate body. The nation of Israel was a type of this body. For this, God went on from Genesis to Exodus, working Himself into the corporate Israel that they would become the house of God, which is God's habitation on earth as typified by the tabernacle in the midst of the Israelites. This corporate Israel was a type of the church as the Body of Christ to be God's dwelling place on earth among men.

Experiencing the Passover,
Having God's Judgment Pass over Them

At that time, the Israelites went down into Egypt and were enslaved by the Egyptians. In order to deliver them from the bondage of Egypt, God had to judge Egypt and smite the firstborn of the Egyptians. To spare the Israelites from the same smiting, God gave them a way of salvation. He commanded them to slaughter the Passover lamb and strike the blood on the lintel and the side posts. Under the covering of the blood, the destroying angel would pass over them and would not smite them (Exo. 12:21-23). But all the firstborn of the land of Egypt were judged by God and were smitten by the destroying angel. In this way, the Israelites were delivered from the enslaving hand of Pharaoh and were freed from Egypt.

Leaving Egypt and Crossing the Red Sea

After the Israelites experienced the Passover, they left Egypt the same night and crossed the Red Sea. This is a type of all the believers in the New Testament, that is, the whole church, experiencing Christ as the Passover and being baptized to be delivered from the world. For the Israelites the experience of the Passover, the exodus from Egypt, and the crossing of the Red Sea were not individual matters but were all corporate matters. They experienced the Passover as a corporate body, they left Egypt as a corporate body, and they crossed the Red Sea as a corporate body. In the eyes of God, we believers are not saved one by one individually. Instead, we enjoy Christ as the redeeming Lamb together, we are baptized together, and we are delivered from the world and saved from this age together. In God there is no difference in time and space. We the believers experience our Passover at the same time, and all of us leave Egypt and cross the Red Sea at the same time.

Passing through the Wilderness to Offer Sacrifices to God

The Israelites were led by God out of Egypt to cross the Red Sea and enter into the wilderness to serve God. Today it is the same for us, the saved ones. We are in the wilderness, away from the bondage of the world, having been released from the enslaving of man and having the true freedom. Here we learn to serve God.

A VIEW FROM THE OLD TESTAMENT TYPES

Experiencing the Bitter Water Turned Sweet

In the journey through the wilderness, God led the Israelites to pass through many experiences. First, they experienced the bitter water turned sweet. The Israelites came to Marah. Because of the bitterness of the water, the people complained to Moses. Jehovah commanded Moses to cast a tree into the water, and the water turned sweet (Exo. 15:25). The bitter water signifies a bitter situation. The tree signifies the cross of Christ. Christians are like the Israelites in the wilderness; often we are confronted with difficulties while journeying on earth. During these times, if we consider the cross of Christ and receive it into us, our bitter situations will turn sweet.

Enjoying the Manna from Heaven as the Daily Supply

The Israelites also enjoyed the manna from heaven as their daily supply. They did not plough nor did they reap in the wilderness. What they ate was the manna from heaven (Exo. 16:15). We who follow the Lord have God's manna from heaven, which is the Lord Jesus. He is the bread of life. When we eat Him, we will not be hungry. He who eats Him will live by Him (John 6:35, 57).

Drinking the Living Water Which Flowed from the Rock

Not only did the Israelites need food in the wilderness; they needed water as well. God solved the problem of their need for food by sending manna, but there was still the need to solve the problem of drinking. For that, God commanded Moses to smite the rock. Out of the rock came water (Exo. 17:6), and their thirst was quenched. Today the Lord Jesus is our manna. He is also our living water. We can drink of Him and be satisfied.

Defeating Amalek

While the Israelites were journeying in the wilderness, Amalek came and fought with them (Exo. 17:8), hindering them from going on. Through the prayer of Moses, the Israelites defeated Amalek. In type, Amalek signifies our flesh. Our flesh is always hindering us from following the Lord. But through the intercession of the Lord Jesus in heaven and through the power of the Holy Spirit, we are enabled to overcome the flesh. Hence, after we have left Egypt and are in the way of following the Lord in the wilderness, there are many needs. The Lord is able to meet all of our needs. He turns the difficulties into sweetness. He satisfies our hunger and quenches our thirst. He overcomes the hindrance of the flesh for us. In this way we can go on fearlessly to the place God has appointed.

Coming to the Mountain Appointed by God, Receiving Revelation, and Erecting the Tabernacle

The Israelites came to Mount Sinai, which was God's appointed place (Exo. 19:1). Here they received the revelation to build the tabernacle so that God would have a dwelling place on earth (Exo. 25:8). Later the tabernacle became the center of the move among the Israelites. This typifies that we the believers are led by the Lord to receive revelation and to build the church as God's dwelling place.

Wandering and Dying in the Wilderness

The Israelites could very well have entered into the good land of Canaan through following the tabernacle had it not been for their evil heart of unbelief which offended God. For that, God was disgusted with that generation. In the end they all died in the wilderness. This typifies the believers wandering and failing in the soul.

Crossing the River Jordan and Entering into Canaan, the Good Land

The Israelites wandered in the wilderness for forty years until a new generation rose up. God brought the new generation through the river Jordan to enter into Canaan. He ordered Joshua to choose twelve men from the people to bring twelve stones from the river Jordan over to the other side. In addition, they set up twelve stones in the river (Josh. 4:2, 8-9). This was done as a symbol that the old Israelites were buried under the river Jordan and that the new Israelites were brought through the river into the good land. This typifies that the believers' natural life passes through the death of Christ, and in resurrection they enjoy Christ as the good land.

Defeating the Enemy, Gaining the Land, and Building the Temple

When the Israelites entered Canaan, God delivered into their hands the people of that land. They were able to defeat the enemy, gain the land, and build the temple of God there. The temple was an enlargement of the tabernacle. It was a dwelling place of God. This typifies that we the believers defeat the spiritual enemies, gain the territory in Christ, and build up the church as God's temple. When we follow Christ, we receive the feeding of the manna, we receive the supply of the living water, and we overcome our flesh by Him. Furthermore, we deny the natural life by passing through the death of Christ, dying and resurrecting together with Him, and enter into Him, being joined together with all the saints to be built up into a solid dwelling place of God in Him.

Becoming Desolate, Failing, and Being Carried Away to Babylon and Returning from Captivity to Jerusalem to Rebuild the Temple of God on the Original Foundation

After the temple was completed, the Israelites gradually became desolate, failed, and were eventually carried away to Babylon to be put under the rule of the Gentiles. After seventy years when the time was completed (2 Chron. 36:11-21), God called them out of Babylon to return to Jerusalem to rebuild the temple on the foundation of the original temple (Ezra 1:3). This typifies the history of the church after it came into being. From Revelation 2—3 we see that the church gradually became desolate, failed, and was carried away to the mysterious Great Babylon, which is the Roman Catholic Church. When the Reformation began during the sixteenth century, the church was delivered from Roman Catholicism back to the original position. Today we are like the returned Israelites, coming out of the mysterious Great Babylon and being recovered to the original ground of the church to rebuild the church of God.

Rebuilding the City of Jerusalem as the Circumference of God's Temple, and Further Rebuilding the Temple and the City of Jerusalem during the Coming Restoration of the Nation of Israel

The Israelites returned, built the temple, and recovered the holy city. When the Lord Jesus comes back again, the nation of Israel will be restored. By then they will rebuild the temple again and will build a bigger Jerusalem. According to Ezekiel 48, the Jerusalem that they will build will have twelve gates and will be their dwelling place with God in the millennium. This typifies the overcomers in the church and the overcoming saints of the Old Testament who will eventually become the New Jerusalem in the millennium. They will be the heavenly part of the millennium and will be the manifestation of the kingdom of the heavens. There they will exercise authority to rule with the Lord Jesus over the nations.

After the one thousand years, this heavenly Jerusalem will be enlarged to become the New Jerusalem in the new heaven and the new earth. She will include all the redeemed ones from all the ages to be the dwelling place and the expression of God in eternity future. She will also become the dwelling place of us, the redeemed ones. Hence, the New Jerusalem in the new heaven and the new earth will become the mutual dwelling place for God and man. God will dwell in the redeemed ones, and the redeemed ones will dwell in God their Redeemer. This New Jerusalem in eternity is the ultimate consummation of the church to be God's eternal expression.

By now, we can clearly see that the history of the nation of Israel is a full type of the history of the church. The history of Israel begins with the Israelites corporately experiencing the Passover during the exodus from Egypt and goes on until the Lord comes back the second time when they will be restored to build the Jerusalem with the twelve gates. The history of the church also began with the Passover, which is the Christ who has been sacrificed (1 Cor. 5:7), and goes on until the millennium with its heavenly Jerusalem which also has twelve gates. Hence, whether it is the Old Testament or the New, in type or by revelation, the whole Bible speaks of the same thing, which is God's economy. The economy of God is the Triune God working Himself into us, the tripartite men. He desires to be man's life, content, and complete supply that man would become God's representation and expression. In the beginning God gained individuals, from Adam through Abel, Enosh, Enoch, Noah, Abraham, Isaac, Jacob, and Joseph. Then God gained a corporate Israel. When we were first saved, seemingly we were individuals; but gradually we feel that we need a corporate Body, which is the church. Because of this we begin to come together for the church life. Today, we are the genuine, real nation of Israel, expressing God as His dwelling place on earth.

I hope you would all see that this is what the Lord is after in His recovery on earth today. First He gains individuals; then He gains a Body. Today we all have our individual experiences; but we are also living a life in the church. It is a life in which the Triune God is joined to the redeemed ones as one spirit. He is our life and content, and we are His rest and habitation. He is our enjoyment, and we are His expression. All these begin with His Spirit mingling with our spirit, continue with the uplifting and the transformation of our soul, and consummate with the uplifting of our body, which is the redemption of our body. Eventually all the redeemed ones will become the New Jerusalem as the mutual dwelling place of God and us and as God's eternal expression. May we all see this vision of God's economy so that we would know how to live in the church and walk in a proper and bright way.

A message given by Brother Witness Lee in Seoul, Korea on November 6, 1988.

CHAPTER THREE

A VIEW OF GOD'S ECONOMY FROM THE NEW TESTAMENT REVELATION

(1)

Scripture Reading: Eph. 3:2-11; 1:9-11

OUTLINE

I. God becoming flesh to bring Himself into man—John 1:14:
   A. Becoming a God-man.
   B. To be experienced by man as grace and reality.
II. This God-man living a human life on earth:
   A. Living and expressing God in the human life—John 6:57a; Acts 10:38.
   B. Experiencing everything of the human life to be qualified as the Captain of salvation and our High Priest—Heb. 2:10, 17-18.
III. This God-man, in the human flesh, accomplishing the all-inclusive death on the cross:
   A. A death which redeemed the sinners—Col. 1:20-22.
   B. A death which released the divine life—John 12:24.
   C. A death which produced the Body of Christ—John 12:24.
   D. A death which created the new man—Eph. 2:15-16.
   E. A death which terminated the old creation—Rom. 6:6.
   F. A death which destroyed Satan—Heb. 2:14.
   G. A death which judged the satanic world of darkness—John 12:31.
IV. This God-man entering into resurrection:

A. Being begotten as the firstborn Son of God, having both divinity and humanity—Acts 13:33.
B. Regenerating the many sons of God, who constitute the church, the Body of Christ—1 Pet. 1:3; Heb. 2:10, 12.
C. Becoming the life-giving Spirit—1 Cor. 15:45b.

V. This God-man, in His resurrection, breathing Himself as the Spirit into His disciples—John 20:22:
A. To be their life and content—Col. 3:4.
B. To be with them forever—John 14:20.
C. To live together with them—John 14:19; Gal. 2:20b.

VI. This God-man, having died and resurrected, ascending to the heavens—Eph. 4:8-12:
A. Bringing with Him the captives whom He took captive out of the hands of Satan.
B. Presenting these captives to God.
C. God giving these captives as gifts to Him, the ascended Head.
D. He, in the position of His ascension, giving these gifts to the church to build up the Body.

A VIEW FROM THE NEW TESTAMENT REVELATION

Prayer: Lord, we worship You for bringing us once again to Your Word. Open and release Your mystery to us that we would see God's eternal economy. Lord, open our hearts and give us a spirit of wisdom and understanding that we would enter into Your heart's desire in a genuine way and would see Your eternal economy. Lord, cleanse us again with Your precious blood, and anoint us again with Your holy anointing oil that both the speaker as well as the listener would enjoy Your presence and touch You. Lord, give us also the utterance to speak forth the fresh words that bear the supply of life and are full of revelation and light. Lord Jesus, we really love Your precious name. We come again to receive You. Supply us that we would all be filled by You to enjoy the riches from on high. May You gain the glory. May we be satisfied and the enemy be shamed. Amen!

In this chapter we want to see God's economy according to the revelation in the New Testament. In the Old Testament, God gave us the types and the pictures. In the New Testament, God gave us the clear words and revelation. The whole New Testament is the revelation of God. There is no need for us to guess or to conjecture. God has already spoken to us the mystery hidden in Him.

We know that God's economy is to work Himself as the Triune God into us, the tripartite men, that we would have His life and nature to become the sons of God and the members of Christ to be constituted the Body of Christ, which is the church, the expression of Christ. This is the goal of God's economy; it is what God has desired throughout the ages. This universal Body also includes those who believe in Christ in all times and all ages. Christ is the Head and we are the Body. He and we together constitute a great universal man. The One who dwells and lives within this great man is the Triune God Himself. He lives in this Body. For this reason, whenever we meet together we feel that God is here, for this is the house of God. Here heaven and earth are joined together, and God and man are joined as one.

We have seen that in eternity past God had a plan, an intention, an arrangement, and an economy. In time He accomplishes this economy step by step. The first step was creation. He created the heavens, the earth, all things, and man. Man is the center of God's creation. Although the heaven is high and the earth is expansive and all the things on it are lovely and beautiful, God considers man as the most precious of them all. This is because man is created in God's image and after His likeness (Gen. 1:26) for the purpose of containing God. Hence, man is after God's kind. Because we as men are after God's kind, God can be grafted into us, and we can be grafted into God. This is what the Lord Jesus meant when He said that He is the vine and we are the branches (John 15:5). When He enters into us, we are grafted into Him.

GOD BECOMING FLESH TO BRING HIMSELF INTO MAN

When did God put Himself into man after He created man? He waited four thousand years. One day in the universe and among mankind a tremendous thing happened. It was something more important than the creation of the heaven and the earth. God became flesh. The God who is the Creator of all things entered into man, being conceived of the Holy Spirit to be born of a virgin. His name was called Jesus. By becoming flesh He brought Himself into man to become a mysterious God-man. He is God, yet He is also man. He is a genuine, proper, and normal man. He was born in Bethlehem, raised in Nazareth, and lived in a poor carpenter's home. At the age of thirty, He came forth to fulfill His commission, working for God and preaching the gospel of God, expressing God before man. His words and deeds often surprised and shocked those who followed Him. Sometimes His words were great yet simple. He said, "I am the light of the world" (John 8:12), "I am the bread that came down out of heaven" (John 6:41), "I am the way, and the reality, and the life" (John 14:6). In human history, there have been many sages and saints. But no one, whether a religious leader or a philosopher, ever said the same things that the Lord Jesus said. Moreover, there are many religions in the world. But no matter what religion it is, those in it are never called the believers in the Lord. Only those believing in Jesus are called the believers in the Lord. This is because only He is the Lord.

A VIEW FROM THE NEW TESTAMENT REVELATION 37

After the Lord's crucifixion and resurrection, He appeared to His disciple, Thomas. When Thomas recognized Him he said, "My Lord and my God!" (John 20:28). No disciple of any person ever calls his teacher this. There is only one Lord in the universe—the Lord Jesus. As the God who created the heavens, the earth, and all the things in it, He has become a man.

The Creator became a God-man with the purpose that man would experience Him as grace and reality (John 1:14). The grace that God gives to man is not something materialistic. Rather, it is the Triune God Himself becoming a man called Jesus to be received by man as his enjoyment. Actually, all things are but dung; only Jesus is the top treasure. To have Jesus is to have the treasure and the grace. But this is not all. He is also the reality. Everything is vanity; all things are a striving after the wind (Eccl. 1:2-14). Only the Triune God is reality. With Him we have eternal life, which makes Him real and experiential to us.

THIS GOD-MAN LIVING A HUMAN LIFE ON EARTH

The Lord Jesus is God becoming a man. He lived on earth for thirty-three and a half years, passing through the storms of the human life and tasting all the bitterness of human living. When He was on earth, He did not have much enjoyment. On the contrary, He was a man of sorrows and acquainted with grief (Isa. 53:3). Everywhere there were difficulties and trials. No one understood Him. But in His human life, He lived out God and expressed God (John 6:57a; Acts 10:38). Moreover, through experiencing everything of the human life, He was qualified to be the Captain of salvation and our High Priest (Heb. 2:10,17-18). He fully satisfied God and is qualified to be our Savior, saving us, solving all of our problems, caring for us, ministering to us, and interceding for us.

THIS GOD-MAN, IN THE HUMAN FLESH, ACCOMPLISHING THE ALL-INCLUSIVE DEATH ON THE CROSS

After the Lord Jesus passed through the test of human living for thirty-three and a half years, He went to the cross according to the appointed time. There He was crucified. He was hanged on the cross for six hours, from nine o'clock in the morning to three o'clock in the afternoon. The first three hours were mainly persecution, ridicule, blasphemy, and reviling from man. The last three hours were mainly judgment from God. God put upon Him the sins of us all. This God-man accomplished an all-inclusive death on the cross in the human flesh. First, this death is a death which redeemed the sinners (Col. 1:20-22). The Lord Jesus was crucified on the cross to redeem us, the sinners, that we may be reconciled to God. Second, His death is a death which released the divine life (John 12:24). His death on the cross was like a grain of wheat that fell into the ground and died. Through the breaking of the shell, the divine life was released. Third, His death is a death which produced the Body of Christ (John 12:24). He, as the unique divine grain that fell to the ground, brought forth many grains. These many grains are mingled together to form a loaf, which is the church, the Body of Christ. Hence, the church is produced out of the death of Christ in the same way that Eve was built out of the rib of Adam when he fell asleep (Gen. 2:21).

Fourth, His death is a death which created the new man (Eph. 2:15-16). Through His death on the cross, Christ abolished the ordinances that caused disharmony between the Jews and the Gentiles and created in Himself out of two one new man. Fifth, His death is a death that terminated the old creation (Rom. 6:6). Our old man, who was created by God and became fallen through sin, is the center of the whole old creation. He is terminated through crucifixion together with Christ. Sixth, His death is a death which annulled Satan (Heb. 2:14). Christ has destroyed the Devil who has the might of death and has made him of no effect. Seventh, His death is a death which judged the satanic world of darkness (John 12:31). When the Lord was lifted up on the cross, not only did He judge Satan, He judged the world, which is hanging upon Satan, as well.

How all-inclusive is the death of Christ! This all-inclusive death which He accomplished on the cross has on the negative side solved all the problems of sin, the old creation, and the world, and on the positive side it released the divine life and produced the new man, the new creation, and the Body of Christ, which is the church.

THIS GOD-MAN ENTERING INTO RESURRECTION

Christ has died and has resurrected. In John 10:18 He said of His life, "No one takes it away from Me, but I lay it down of Myself. I have authority to lay it down, and I have authority to take it again." On the one hand, He suffered the pain of death. On the other hand, He entered death to have a tour of Hades. Because death could not hold Him down, He came out of death and entered into resurrection. In resurrection He was begotten the firstborn Son of God, with both the divine nature and the human nature (Acts 13:33). In eternity Christ was the only begotten Son of God, with divinity only, having no humanity with Him. After He became flesh, He put on humanity. But at that time, His humanity only qualified Him to be the Son of Man, not the Son of God. After passing through death and resurrection, He was begotten the firstborn Son of God, and His humanity was uplifted into His divinity. Now He is no longer just the only begotten Son of God; He is also the firstborn Son of God. As the only begotten Son of God, He has divinity only. As the firstborn Son of God, He has both divinity and humanity.

When we say that Christ is the firstborn Son of God, it means that He has many brothers. Through the resurrection of Christ, God has regenerated us, the believers, to become the sons of God (1 Pet. 1:3). From the view of God's economy, when the Lord Jesus resurrected, we were resurrected together with Him (Eph. 2:5-6). He was begotten the firstborn Son of God, and we were begotten the many sons of God. In Christ's resurrection, He was begotten, and we also were begotten. Paul was begotten then, Martin Luther was begotten then, and all of us were also begotten then.

Furthermore, in His resurrection Christ became the life-giving Spirit (1 Cor. 15:45b). Because of this, He can enter into His many brothers to be their life and life supply that they may share with Him the same life and the same nature and may become one spirit with Him. This is God's economy.

THIS GOD-MAN, IN HIS RESURRECTION, BREATHING HIMSELF AS THE SPIRIT INTO HIS DISCIPLES

On the evening of the Lord's resurrection, the disciples hid themselves behind closed doors for fear of the Jews. But Jesus came and stood in the midst of them, saying, "Peace be to you." After this, He breathed into them and said, "Receive the Holy Spirit" (John 20:19-22). This Holy Spirit is the Lord Himself. When He breathed into His disciples, He was breathing Himself as the Holy Spirit into them. From that time on, the Lord as the Holy Spirit was in the disciples to be their life and content (Col. 3:4), being with them forever (John 14:20; Matt. 28:20), and living together with them (John 14:19; Gal. 2:20b).

After these things, the disciples went down to the sea to fish, and the Lord appeared to them again. He trained them once more to become accustomed to His invisible presence. It was not His coming; rather, it was His appearing. Whether or not they felt His presence, the Lord was with them all the time. Because of their weakness, the Lord sometimes manifested His presence to them to strengthen their faith in Him. Today, He is the same to us. Since He is the Spirit, there is an invisible presence within us. Whether or not we feel it, He is still with us. Sometimes He appears. Sometimes He disappears. Neither His appearing nor His disappearing is according to us. But whether He appears or disappears, He is with us all the time. Our Lord is such a wonderful One today. Hence, we who believe in Christ are a peculiar people. Sometimes without any reason we are overflowing with joy, praying and singing. At other times, we are despondent and downcast, sighing and sorrowing. When we feel the Lord's presence, everything is good. When we do not feel the Lord's presence, we lose our bearing, and discouragement, murmurings, and temper all appear. But once we touch the Lord Jesus, we feel once more that He is so faithful and lovable, and all the problems are blown away like clouds. All these are due to the fact that we have a wonderful Lord within us.

THIS GOD-MAN, HAVING DIED AND RESURRECTED, ASCENDING TO THE HEAVENS

As the God-man who has died and resurrected, the Lord Jesus has not only become the life-giving Spirit to enter into the disciples, but He has also ascended to the heavens. Ephesians 4:8-12 tells us that in His resurrection and ascension, the Lord Jesus led a train of conquered captives. These captives are we, the redeemed saints. Before we were saved, we were the captives of Satan, bound in sin and death. Through His death and resurrection, Christ has destroyed Satan and has captured us out of the hands of Satan unto Himself. In His ascension, He took these captives and presented them before God. God in turn gave these captives back as gifts to the ascended Head. In the position of His ascension, He gave these gifts to the church. These gifts—among whom are some apostles, prophets, evangelists, and shepherds and teachers—perfect all the saints in the church that the saints would all function to participate in the work of the ministry, which is the building up of the Body of Christ. In the end, God will have a church that satisfies His heart's desire, and Christ will have a built up Body. This is what God will accomplish in His economy in this age.

A message given by Brother Witness Lee in Seoul, Korea on November 6, 1988.

Chapter Four

A VIEW OF GOD'S ECONOMY
FROM THE NEW TESTAMENT REVELATION

(2)

Scripture Reading: Eph. 3:2-11; 1:9-11

OUTLINE

VII. The ascended God-man as the Head in His ascension:
  A. Pouring out the Holy Spirit as the ultimate consummation of the Triune God, the realization and reality of Him as the Head, upon all His believers throughout all the ages and among all the nations—Acts 2:1-4, 33.
  B. Baptizing them into one Body, the church—1 Cor. 12:13a.

VIII. The church being given to drink of Him as the Spirit and becoming one Spirit with Him—1 Cor. 12:13b; 6:17:
  A. Enjoying His all-inclusive Spirit as the life supply—Phil. 1:19.
  B. Receiving gifts from Him to function as members of His Body—Rom. 12:4-8.

IX. The church as the Body of Christ being expressed as the local churches in all the localities to be the golden lampstands shining forth Christ—Rev. 1:11-12, 20b:
  A. In administrative affairs, being administered locally.
  B. In life, nature, and testimony, being the unique Body of Christ in the whole universe—Eph. 4:3-6; 1 Cor. 12:12.

C. Having the sevenfold intensified Spirit of Christ for the strengthening of the shining of the golden lampstands—Rev. 1:4; 4:5; 5:6.
X. The failure of the church:
  A. Becoming desolate and degraded—Rev. 2:14-15, 20.
  B. Being carried away to the mysterious Great Babylon—Rev. 17:5.
XI. The recovery of the church:
  A. Leaving the Great Babylon—Rev. 18:4.
  B. Returning to the original ground of the church, recovering the normal church life—Rev. 3:1, 4, 7-12.
XII. The overcomers in the church and the overcomers among the Old Testament saints eventually constituting:
  A. The bride of Christ—Rev. 19:7-9.
  B. The army of Christ, with Christ defeating Antichrist and his army—Rev. 17:12-14; 19:19-20.
  C. The New Jerusalem in the millennium, as the manifestation of the kingdom of the heavens, reigning with Christ to shepherd the nations—Rev. 3:12; 20:4, 6; 2:26-27.
XIII. All the saints in the church and those in the Old Testament ultimately becoming the New Jerusalem in the new heaven and new earth—Rev. 21:1-2, 12, 14:
  A. As the mutual dwelling place for God and His redeemed in eternity—Rev. 21:3, 22.
  B. As the full expression of God for eternity—Rev. 21:10-11, 23-24.

We have seen the first part of God's New Testament economy, which is mainly concerning the Lord Jesus. The economy of God is the Triune God working Himself into tripartite men that they may become the members of Christ to be constituted the Body of Christ. This economy of God is to be fulfilled not only in this age but also in eternity.

According to the revelation of the New Testament, the first step God took in order to accomplish His economy was that He Himself became the flesh. Through this He became a wonderful God-man, being at the same time God as well as man. In the universe, God has two special kinds of creatures: angels and human beings. The angels belong to the heavens, and man belongs to the earth. If it were up to us, we would probably choose to be an angel. When I was young, I also would have chosen to be an angel. To be an angel is too good. He can live in heaven freely, having in addition the authority of God. But it is so troublesome to be a human being. There are many distractions and sufferings. But after being a Christian for sixty years, having gained a more thorough understanding of the Bible, having realized God's economy, and having had some experience, I have to say that I do not want to be an angel. Rather, I like being a man. Only man is the object of God's economy. The angels are but the slaves who minister unto man (Heb. 1:14). Even the God of creation one day became a man for the purpose of accomplishing His economy. This man was Jesus Christ. He lived on the earth for thirty-three and a half years. He was in the same manner as man, with the human life and human nature, having the need to eat, drink, and sleep, and even being able to shed tears.

When He was thirty years of age, He came out to fulfill His ministry. He came to the shore of the sea of Galilee and called the two brothers, Peter and Andrew, saying, "Follow Me." They immediately dropped their nets and followed Him (Matt. 4:18-20). At that time, the Lord had not yet entered into them. During the three years or more when Peter was following the Lord, most of the time he spoke and acted by himself. One time he received the revelation from the Father and recognized Jesus as the Christ, the Son of the living God. But not long after that, when the Lord Jesus unveiled to His disciples His need to be crucified and resurrected, Peter, in minding the things of man instead of the things of God, became the mouthpiece of Satan and was a stumbling block to the Lord (Matt. 16:16-23). On His last journey to Jerusalem, the Lord Jesus unveiled once more to His disciples His crucifixion and resurrection. Not only did they miss those words, but they were on the contrary arguing among themselves who should be the greatest among them (Matt. 20:17-28). On the night that the Lord Jesus was betrayed, He said to them, "You will all be stumbled in Me this night, for it is written, I will smite the Shepherd, and the sheep of the flock shall be scattered....But Peter answered and said to Him, If all shall be stumbled in You, I will never be stumbled. Jesus said to him, Truly I say to you, that this night, before a cock crows, you will deny Me three times" (Matt. 26:31-35). Later, Peter did deny the Lord three times before men; then the cock crowed. Peter thought of the Lord Jesus' word and went out and wept (Matt. 26:69-75).

Even by that time, Peter still did not have the Lord Jesus within him. It was not until the Lord Jesus was crucified and resurrected and became a life-giving Spirit. On the evening of the day of His resurrection, He came in the midst of the disciples and said to them, "Peace be to you." Then He breathed into them and said to them, "Receive the Holy Spirit." The Spirit which they received was the resurrected Lord Himself. From that day on, the Lord Jesus entered into Peter as well as all those who believed in Him. After the Lord ascended to heaven, the disciples went back to Jerusalem. There about a hundred and twenty of them gathered together in an upper room and persevered in prayer with one accord. After ten days, when Pentecost arrived, the Holy Spirit was poured out. Peter stood up with the eleven apostles and preached the gospel to all those dwelling in Jerusalem. Peter was no longer the Peter of the past. He was changed. This is because the Lord who had died and resurrected had entered into him to be his life and everything (Acts 1:12-15; 2:1-14).

This shows us clearly that when God became flesh, He lived the human life for thirty-three and a half years, experiencing all the sufferings and trials. In His human life, He lived out God and expressed God among men. He passed through everything of the human life and was qualified to be man's Savior. But He still could not enter into man. Hence, He had to go to the cross to accomplish the all-inclusive death so that He could solve all the negative problems in the universe and could release the divine life. After this, He rose from the dead to become the life-giving Spirit and breathed Himself into the disciples to become their life and content. In ascension, He gave them as gifts to the church for the building up of the Body of Christ. These six items—God's becoming flesh, His human living, His crucifixion, His resurrection, His breathing into the disciples, and His ascension—constitute the major steps God took for the fulfillment of His New Testament economy.

In this chapter we will go on from the foregoing six major items to see God's economy from the New Testament revelation. The first six items concern the Lord's work on earth. Starting from the seventh point, all the items concern the Lord's work in heaven.

THE ASCENDED GOD-MAN
AS THE HEAD IN HIS ASCENSION

In His ascension, the Lord Jesus as the ascended God-man, as the Head, poured out the Holy Spirit as the ultimate consummation of the Triune God, the realization and reality of Him as the Head, upon all His believers throughout all the ages and among all the nations (Acts 2:1-4, 33) and baptized them once for all into one Body, the church (1 Cor. 12:13a). Hence, on the day of Pentecost, the Body of Christ, the church, was brought into being through the outpouring of the Holy Spirit.

THE CHURCH BEING GIVEN TO DRINK
OF HIM AS THE SPIRIT AND
BECOMING ONE SPIRIT WITH HIM

When the church, which is composed of all the saved ones throughout all the ages and among all the nations, was baptized by this one Spirit into one Body, she was at the same time made to drink of this one Spirit (1 Cor. 12:13b).

Whenever we call "O Lord Jesus," we are drinking of this Holy Spirit. If we call daily and hourly, we will drink of this Spirit daily and hourly. We call on the Lord, but we receive the Holy Spirit. Jesus is the name, and the Holy Spirit is the person. When we call on the Lord, the Holy Spirit comes, and we drink of this Spirit. This is not all. We also become one spirit with Him (1 Cor. 6:17). In this way, we can enjoy this all-inclusive Spirit as the life supply (Phil. 1:19). When we rise up in the morning, if we do not call on the Lord and drink of the Holy Spirit to the full, we will be empty, weak, and impotent throughout the day. But if we call on the Lord and drink of the Holy Spirit as soon as we rise up, we will surely be full of the Spirit and supplied with life to be full of strength the whole day long. Furthermore, we will receive the gifts from Him to function as the members of His Body (Rom. 12:4-8). All the members of the Body of Christ will receive gifts through the supply of life and will manifest their functions. This is the church.

Hebrews 8:1-2 and 9:11-12 tell us that after Christ ascended, He passed through the greater and more perfect tabernacle and became a Minister of the holy places. First, He poured out the all-inclusive Spirit to produce the church. Second, in His position of ascension, He gave gifts to the church. Third, He ministers the life supply from heaven into the believers that they may receive the enjoyment to function as members. Fourth, as our High Priest, He cares for us, takes care of our needs, and makes supplication for us that we may experience Him and receive the heavenly supply to live the heavenly life.

THE CHURCH AS THE BODY OF CHRIST BEING EXPRESSED AS THE LOCAL CHURCHES IN ALL THE LOCALITIES TO BE THE GOLDEN LAMPSTANDS SHINING FORTH CHRIST

If there is a group of believers in a place who have the life of God and always call on the Lord, drink of the Holy Spirit, and enjoy the heavenly supply, and who subsequently receive gifts to function, they are the church as a golden lampstand shining forth Christ. The golden lampstands are the churches in the various localities showing forth the testimony of Christ. On the one hand, these churches in the various localities are administered locally in their administrative affairs. For example, it is up to the church in Seoul to decide where and how they should meet as the church in Seoul. In the same way, it is up to the church in Inchon to decide where and how the church in Inchon should meet. Every church has its particular condition and needs; no two places are the same. Concerning these administrative matters, there is no uniformity; every place is administered locally. On the other hand, in life, nature, and testimony, there is the unique Body in the universe (Eph. 4:3-6; 1 Cor. 12:12). This is why the seven golden lampstands in Revelation 1:11-12, 20b are the same in nature and shape. They are all lampstands made of pure gold. Moreover, the testimony they bear and the light they shine forth are all the same. There is no distinction among them. Whether in nature, function, or testimony, the church in each locality and all the churches on the whole earth should be the same. Furthermore, in this dark age the church has the sevenfold intensified Spirit of Christ for the intensification of the shining of the golden lampstands (Rev. 1:4; 4:5; 5:6). At the time when John was writing the book of Revelation, the churches had degraded, and the age had become dark. This is why God's move and work on earth required the sevenfold intensified Spirit of God. The situation is the same today. Therefore, we all need to be filled with this sevenfold intensified Spirit, that the shining of the golden lampstands would become brighter and brighter.

THE FAILURE OF THE CHURCH

From the Bible we see that soon after the age of the apostles the local churches as the golden lampstands became desolate, degraded, and fallen (Rev. 2:14-15, 20) and were carried away to the mysterious Great Babylon (Rev. 17:5); this is similar to the Israelites in the Old Testament who were taken captive into Babylon through their degradation and failure. This mysterious Great Babylon is the apostate Roman Catholic Church. According to church history, this period lasted for at least ten centuries from about A.D. 570 to about

A.D. 1500 at the time of Luther's Reformation. This was also the period known in world history as the Dark Ages.

THE RECOVERY OF THE CHURCH

At the time of the Reformation, the church had a recovery. She left the apostate Roman Catholic Church (Rev. 18:4) and gradually returned to the original ground of oneness to have the proper church life (Rev. 3:1, 4, 7-12). This is the Lord's call for the overcomers in the degraded and desolate church, as recorded in Revelation 2—3. Today we are in the church of the Lord's recovery. Whether we are in Korea, China, or the West, we have returned to the local ground of oneness and expect to be recovered continuously back to the normal church life, which is a life of inwardly being filled by the Spirit and outwardly living Christ, loving one another, fellowshipping one with another, and fellowshipping with the Triune God.

THE OVERCOMERS IN THE CHURCH AND THE OVERCOMERS AMONG THE OLD TESTAMENT SAINTS BEING EVENTUALLY CONSTITUTED

First, the overcomers in the church and the overcomers among the Old Testament saints are constituted the bride of Christ (Rev. 19:7-9). This bride is the spouse of Christ, sharing with Christ His kingly rule in the coming millennium. Second, these overcomers throughout the ages will constitute the army of Christ at His return who with Christ will defeat Antichrist and his army (Rev. 17:12-14; 19:19-20). Third, they will constitute the New Jerusalem in the millennium. The New Jerusalem will appear in two stages. The first stage will appear in the millennium; the second stage will appear in the new heaven and new earth in eternity. The New Jerusalem in the millennium includes only the overcoming saints throughout the ages; it does not include the saints who fail and must therefore pass through God's dealing to be further perfected. This is like going to school. Those who fail in the final examination cannot graduate; they must have make-up lessons. Only after they pass through those lessons can they graduate. Therefore, if you are lazy and loose as a Christian today and do not grow in life, you will be considered a failing one when Jesus comes back again. The overcoming saints will reign and rejoice with the Lord in the millennium while you will be there "making up your lessons," being dealt with and chastised by God until you mature. The New Jerusalem in the millennium, which is constituted of the overcoming saints throughout the ages, will be the manifestation of the kingdom of the heavens. There the overcoming ones will reign with Christ to shepherd the nations (Rev. 3:12; 20:4, 6; 2:26-27).

ALL THE SAINTS IN THE CHURCH AND IN THE OLD TESTAMENT, ULTIMATELY BECOMING THE NEW JERUSALEM IN THE NEW HEAVEN AND NEW EARTH

After the millennium, there will be a new heaven and new earth. By that time, it will not just be the overcomers who will be there. The church and the Old Testament saints, including all the ones who will have been perfected and will be mature, will all become the New Jerusalem in the new heaven and new earth. Those saints who fail now will also be mature at that time after God's dealing and perfecting for a thousand years. They will also have a part in the New Jerusalem. This expanded New Jerusalem will be the mutual dwelling place for God and His redeemed people in eternity (Rev. 21:3, 22). On the one hand, she will be God's tabernacle, His dwelling place. On the other hand, she will be the temple of God, the dwelling place for all those who serve Him. At the same time, this New Jerusalem is the corporate, expanded Christ as the eternal full expression of God. John 1:14 says, "And the Word became flesh [who is Jesus Christ] and tabernacled among us." In this miniature tabernacle God lived within and was expressed without. In the new heaven and new earth in eternity, all the saved saints throughout the ages will have been perfected by God. They will be fully mingled with the Triune God to become an expanded tabernacle. This expanded tabernacle will be the mutual dwelling place for God and His redeemed people and will become the full, complete, and ultimate expression of God unto eternity. This is the ultimate completion of God's economy.

In between the miniature tabernacle of Jesus and the

expanded tabernacle of the New Jerusalem is God's church on earth today. Every local church should be such a tabernacle, filled with God within and expressing God without. Every one of us in the local church should live this life of the tabernacle that God would have a dwelling place on earth and we would also dwell within it. In this way, God will be expressed in every place. Hallelujah! This is God's economy.

A message given by Brother Witness Lee in Seoul, Korea on November 7, 1988.

CHAPTER FIVE

THE BUILDING UP OF THE BODY OF CHRIST

(1)

Scripture Reading: Matt. 16:18; Eph. 4:8-14

OUTLINE

I. Christ's prophecy—Matt. 16:18:
  A. "On this rock [Christ and the revelation of Christ received by the apostles] I will build My church."
  B. "The gates of Hades shall not prevail against it."
II. Christ as the ascended Head giving gifts to men—Eph. 4:8-11:
  A. Some apostles:
    1. Those who have received the revelation of God's New Testament economy concerning Christ and the church—Matt. 16:16-18; Gal. 1:11-12, 15-16; Eph. 3:3-4, 8-11; 5:32.
    2. Those who are able to preach the gospel of Christ to save the sinners chosen and called by God, bringing them unto Christ—Gal. 1:16a; Eph. 3:8; 2 Cor. 11:2.
    3. Those who are able to establish local churches and to appoint in them the elders for leading, shepherding, teaching, and overseeing—Acts 14:23; 1 Tim. 5:17; 1 Pet. 5:2.
    4. Those who are able to determine doctrines, to release the truth, to perfect the saints, and to build up the Body of Christ—1 Tim. 2:7; Eph. 4:11-12.

B. Some prophets—speaking for the Lord, speaking forth the Lord, and speaking the Lord into men—1 Cor. 14:1, 4-5, 23a, 24-26, 31.
C. Some evangelists—preaching Christ and the unsearchable riches of Christ as the gospel to save the desolate sinners, bringing them unto Christ.
D. Some shepherds and teachers—shepherding and teaching the believers.
E. For the perfecting of the saints unto the work of ministry—the building up of the Body of Christ, that the saints may arrive at—Eph. 4:12-14:
   1. The oneness of the faith and of the full knowledge of the Son of God.
   2. A full-grown man.
   3. The measure of the stature of the fullness of Christ.
   4. No longer being babes tossed by waves and carried about by the winds of teachings.

From this message forward, we will consider the building up of the Body of Christ. Here I am not speaking concerning the building up of the local churches. Rather, I am speaking concerning the building up of the Body of Christ. The local churches are local—they are in the different localities and are plural in number. Today on the whole earth, over the six continents, there are about eleven hundred churches in the Lord's recovery. But the Body of Christ is unique in the whole universe. There is only one Body. All the local churches in all times and places are part of this unique Body of Christ.

CHRIST'S PROPHECY

Building the Church on This Rock

The Lord prophesied in Matthew 16 that He would build His church, which is His Body, upon this rock. On the one hand, this rock signifies Christ; on the other hand, it signifies the revelation seen by the apostles. The Bible shows us that, on the one hand, the Body of Christ is built upon Christ Himself, with Him as the foundation (1 Cor. 3:11). On the other hand, it is built upon the foundation of the apostles and the prophets (Eph. 2:20). The foundation of the apostles and the prophets is the revelation they have seen, which is the whole New Testament, from Matthew to Revelation.

The church is mentioned for the first time in the whole Bible in Matthew 16. Although there are several types in the Old Testament typifying the church, the word "church" is not found in the Old Testament. Therefore, in the Old Testament the church is a mystery hidden in God. None of the ones such as Adam, Noah, Abraham, Moses, David, or Isaiah knew about this. The Old Testament saints did not know why they were fearing and worshipping God and why God was caring for them; they only knew that the Messiah, the Christ, would come. They earnestly expected Him to come to establish the kingdom of the heavens on earth. They did not know that God wanted to obtain a church as the Body of Christ. In the New Testament, John the Baptist appeared, calling people to repent and to believe in the gospel. The Lord Jesus continued what John had preached, and as a result, Peter, James, John, and many others received it. Of these, the Lord appointed twelve as apostles and sent them out to preach the gospel, but none of them knew that all this was for the church. I believe by the time they came to Matthew 16, the disciples had been following the Lord for about two to three years. At that time the Lord brought them out of Jerusalem and the land of Judea, away from the holy city, the holy temple, the sacrifice, the incense, and the places full of religious atmosphere, to the region of Caesarea Philippi in the north, at the foot of a mountain by the border of the land of Judea. There the Lord asked them, "Who do you say that I am?" Peter answered and said, "You are the Christ, the Son of the living God" (v. 16). This time he did not say foolish things; his sky was clear, without clouds. He received the revelation and saw that according to His ministry, the Lord Jesus is God's Anointed for the fulfillment of God's purpose, and that according to His person, He is the Son of God, the embodiment of God. Here Peter uttered some stunning words. Immediately the Lord told him that this was not revealed to him by man but by God the Father. Furthermore, the Lord said, "On this rock I will build My church" (v. 18). In this word the Lord showed Peter that it is not enough just to know Him as the Christ; Peter must also know that upon Him He will build the church. Christ is only the Head; He needs a Body, which is the church, to be His match. The Head and the Body cannot be divided; Christ and the church is a great mystery (Eph. 5:32). Not only must we know Christ; we must know the church as well.

It has now been nearly two thousand years since the time of Christ's ascension. The greatest thing that has happened during this time is the producing of the church. What we are doing here today is to "stir up" churches. To say that we are building up the church means that we are "stirring up" churches. What were Peter and Paul doing? They were stirring up churches! What were the Western missionaries doing when they left their countries and kinsmen and crossed the ocean? They were stirring up churches! At present, Christ on the throne in heaven is sending His seven Spirits to enliven us. For what purpose? For the purpose of stirring up churches everywhere, until the whole world is so stirred up that it is filled with churches! The Lord said that the gospel of the kingdom shall be preached in the whole inhabited earth and then the end shall come. Today the end has not yet come, because the gospel has not yet been preached in the whole inhabited earth, and the whole earth has not yet been filled with churches. You have heard that there is the gospelizing work in Taiwan. This gospelizing work also includes the "church-izing" work. We hope that by the end of 1991, every town and village in Taiwan will have a church. Thank the Lord! In Korea there are about three thousand brothers and sisters who are willing to offer themselves to the Lord to "stir up" churches here. I believe that after five years the situation in Korea will be changed, and all the places will be filled with churches!

The Gates of Hades Not Being Able to Prevail against the Church

In Matthew 16:18 the Lord continued by saying, "the gates of Hades shall not prevail against it [the church]." The gates of Hades is the authority of Satan's darkness; it is also the authority of death. However, it cannot prevail against the church, for the church is the Body of Christ, the Head, who sits on the throne in heaven. All authority in heaven and on earth is given to Christ. Since the church is His Body, the gates of Hades cannot prevail against the church. This ascended Head has already been crowned with glory and honor on the throne (Heb. 2:9). He has also received authority from God the Father and has been made Lord and Christ (Acts 2:36) and the Ruler of the kings of the earth (Rev. 1:5). Now He operates by His Spirit, which is the sevenfold intensified Spirit (Rev. 4:5; 5:6), to apply all that He has accomplished and obtained to us for the building up of His Body. This is the work of Christ in heaven. Heaven, where He is, is joined to our spirit. The spirit within us is linked to heaven. The book of Genesis in the Old Testament records the story of Jacob when he dreamed of a heavenly ladder in the wilderness. On the ladder there were angels of God ascending and descending (Gen. 28:12). The heavenly ladder is a type of the ascended

Christ. The place where the ladder was set up was called Bethel, and it was the gate of heaven (Gen. 28:18-19). Hebrews 4:16 tells us that we can come boldly to the throne of grace. We are now living on earth. How then can we come to God's throne in heaven? The key is the spirit mentioned in verse 12 of Hebrews 4. The Christ who is sitting on the throne in heaven is now also in us (Rom. 8:10), that is, in our spirit (2 Tim. 4:22). God's dwelling place is this spirit. Bethel is the house of God, the habitation of God, and the gate of heaven. There Christ is the ladder, linking earth to heaven and bringing heaven down to earth. Since our spirit now is God's dwelling place, this spirit is the gate of heaven. Here Christ is the ladder, joining us, the people on earth, to heaven and bringing heaven to us.

Sometimes when you wake up in the morning, you feel very weak. But when you call "O Lord Jesus," immediately the ascended Christ will be transmitted into you like electricity, and you will be strengthened within. Sometimes you feel tired and do not want to come to the meetings. But as soon as you say softly within, "Lord!" something will start moving within you, and you will end up coming to the meeting. The more you come to the meetings, the more you will be joined to heaven, and the stronger you will become. All the tiredness will be gone. This is Christ bringing heaven to us within, enabling us to overcome Satan's might of death.

CHRIST AS THE ASCENDED HEAD
GIVING GIFTS TO MEN

Ephesians 4:8-11 shows us that this ascended Head gave gifts to men. After Christ ascended, He first gave some gifted persons to the church. These gifted persons are people who "stir up" churches and also perfect others to "stir up" more churches.

Some Apostles

The ascended Head gave four kinds of gifts. The first class is the apostles (Eph. 4:11). These apostles receive the revelation of God's New Testament economy concerning Christ and the church (Matt. 16:16-18; Gal. 1:11-12, 15-16; Eph. 3:3-4,

8-11; 5:32). First, they receive the revelation, and the revelation makes their spirits burning and causes them to forget about themselves. They then go out to preach the revelation that others may also be burned. These apostles also preach the gospel of Christ to save the sinners chosen and called by God, bringing them to Christ (Gal. 1:16a; Eph. 3:8; 2 Cor. 11:2). They do not preach the superficial gospel, one that tells people about going to heaven instead of hell; rather, they preach to others the all-inclusive Christ as the gospel. Furthermore, the apostles are able to establish local churches and to appoint in them the elders for leading, shepherding, teaching, and overseeing (Acts 14:23; 1 Tim. 5:17; 1 Pet. 5:2). They are also able to determine doctrines, to release the truth, to perfect the saints, and to build up the Body of Christ (1 Tim. 2:7; Eph. 4:11-12). These are the four things that an apostle should do.

Some Prophets

The prophets are the second class of gifts given by the ascended Christ (Eph. 4:11). The prophets are those who through the Lord's revelation, speak for the Lord, speak forth the Lord, and speak the Lord into others. Sometimes they are also moved to utter some predictions. For the perfecting of the saints and the building up of the Body of Christ, they are second only to the apostles and are a very important class of people.

Some Evangelists

The evangelists are the third class of persons given by the ascended Head. They can preach Christ and the unsearchable riches of Christ as the gospel to save the desolate sinners, bringing them to Christ.

Some Shepherds and Teachers

The shepherds and teachers are the fourth class of persons given by the ascended Head. According to the grammatical structure in Greek, the shepherds and teachers here refer to one class of gifted persons. The shepherds should know how to teach others, and the teachers should also know how to feed others. They are able to shepherd and teach the believers and are also able to feed the new ones in the same way that a mother feeds, shepherds, leads, and teaches her children.

For the Perfecting of the Saints unto the Work of Ministry

The four classes of persons—the apostles, the prophets, the evangelists, and the shepherds and teachers—preach the gospel to save others on the one hand. On the other hand, they raise up churches in the localities. Then they also feed, shepherd, and teach the saints. Furthermore, among these saints they speak for the Lord and speak the Lord into them. In this way all the saints are perfected. The meaning of perfecting can be illustrated by university students being taught by professors of different subjects. After four years of studying, they graduate and are able to do the same things that the professors do; they have all been perfected. Christ as the Head gave these four kinds of gifts to the church for the purpose of perfecting the saints that the latter may also be the apostles, the prophets, the evangelists, and the shepherds and teachers. Unfortunately this is not the case in the existing system of Christianity. It only trains some preachers to gather a congregation on Sunday for a service where one speaks and the rest listen. Most of them after listening for decades still have not received much perfecting.

In the Lord's recovery, all the gifts such as the apostles, the prophets, the evangelists, and the shepherds and teachers should do the work of perfecting. In other words, they should all do the work of training. They should be like the professors perfecting the students. In this way, after a few years, the saints will be perfected and will be able to do the work that they do. At present, the publications among us are very rich and numerous. There are at least four thousand different messages. If you would spend the time, these materials are very good to help you be perfected. I heard that you have translated all the Life-study Messages of the New Testament into Korean. If you would spend two hours every day for two years to read these Life-study Messages, you will be equipped. In four years' time you will be able to finish all of these messages.

At the same time, you are in the church seeing how the apostles raise up churches, how they appoint elders, how they preach the high gospel, how they bring people into Christ to enjoy the riches of Christ, and how they determine doctrines. For example, someone asked me this morning about the difference between the denominations and the church. In a simple word, first, the denominations are denominated; they have divided the Body of Christ. The church is not denominated; it is one. All the believers, whether they are sprinkled or immersed, are in the church as long as they are saved. Second, the denominations do not have a definite ground. The church, however, has a definite ground which is also the unique ground. Here we stand on the ground of oneness in the different localities to worship God together and to build up the Body of Christ together. I believe that after five years many of you will be able to be apostles, preaching the gospel from city to city and from village to village, establishing churches, releasing the truth, and building up the Body of Christ.

Next are the prophets. The present atmosphere in the church meetings is that you are being trained to speak for the Lord. For example, the sharings after a message are mostly repetitions of words that you just heard. After speaking this way for a while, you will be able to speak for the Lord. Perhaps the first time you stand up you are afraid to speak, and you are scared. But as long as you keep practicing, your boldness will increase, and your voice will get stronger. Gradually you will not only be able to speak for the Lord, but you will also be able to speak forth the Lord and to speak the Lord into others. After the meetings, people may not remember much about the messages they heard. But they will feel that there is One following them all the time. The reason for this is that you have spoken the Lord into them. After you return home, do not only chat with your family; instead you must learn to speak the Lord's word to your family, to speak forth the Lord, and to speak the Lord into them. In this way they will discover that you have changed, and they will also change through your speaking. This is to prophesy. Paul said in 1 Corinthians 14 that you can all prophesy one by one (v. 31).

The evangelists' perfecting of the saints makes every saint burdened with a spirit for the gospel. It cheers and warms up the gospel atmosphere for the saints that they would become burning to preach the gospel. In preaching the gospel it also helps them to speak to the point, not deviating from the subject. While they speak, the listeners' hearts, mouths, and spirits will all be open and they will receive the Lord to be saved. The shepherds and teachers' perfecting is like perfecting people to be mothers. Many brothers and sisters cannot feed people after they have been brought to salvation. They are like the mother who cannot nurse her child; thus the new ones do not receive much supply and teaching. Hence, we all have to be shepherds perfecting others, and we all have to learn. The more we do these things, the more we will improve, and the better we will become at doing them.

In the end, after this kind of perfecting, the saints will be able to be the apostles, the prophets, the evangelists, and the shepherds and teachers. Every member will be able to function and will participate in the work of the New Testament ministry, which is the building up of the Body of Christ, until we all arrive at the oneness of the faith and of the full knowledge of the Son of God, at a full-grown man, and at the measure of the stature of the fullness of Christ. In this way we will no longer be babes tossed by waves and carried about by the winds of teachings. The whole church will grow into a mature man with the stature of Christ. This is the building up of the Body of Christ.

A message given by Brother Witness Lee in Seoul, Korea on November 7, 1988.

Chapter Six

THE BUILDING UP
OF THE BODY OF CHRIST

(2)

Scripture Reading: Eph. 4:15-16

OUTLINE

III. The perfected saints directly building up the Body of Christ—Eph. 4:15-16:
  A. Holding to truth in love:
    1. God's New Testament economy.
    2. The all-inclusive Christ.
    3. The church as the Body of Christ—an organism.
  B. Growing into Christ the Head in all things:
    1. Through acknowledging the headship of Christ.
    2. Letting Christ increase and grow in us, His members, in every inward part.
  C. Out from the Head:
    1. All the Body causing the growth of the Body of Christ:
      a. Through every joint of the supply—every specially gifted part of the Body of Christ for the supplying of every member of the Body of Christ.
      b. And through the operation in measure of each one part (each member of the Body of Christ).
    2. All the Body being built together:

a. Being fitted together—all parts of the frame being fitted together into one structure.
b. Being knit together—all the other parts being joined to the frame and knit together into one Body.
3. The Body of Christ building itself up:
   a. In love—in the element and sphere of the divine love.
   b. A direct building up—all the members of the Body of Christ directly building up the Body of Christ.

THE BUILDING UP OF THE BODY OF CHRIST

Ephesians 4:12-16 occupies a special place in the New Testament because it shows us the mystery concerning the building up of the Body of Christ. Without these few verses, we would not know how to build up the Body of Christ. First, we must say that to build up the Body of Christ is not to build up a congregation. A congregation is an organization, but the Body of Christ is an organism. An organism is altogether a matter of life, whereas an organization has no life. For example, a table is framed together from pieces of wood. It is just an organization; it does not have any life within. A robot may do all kinds of things, but it is still an organization; it has no life. On the contrary, I stand here not as an organization but as an organism. My whole being is a story of life; every part of me is of life. Some think that since the church is a congregation, it must be an organization. However, immediately after Paul mentioned the church in Ephesians 1:22, he said in verse 23 that the church is the Body of Christ. Some Bible expositors have considered the Body of Christ to be a metaphor. But the Bible says explicitly that the church is the Body of Christ. It is not a metaphor, but a fact. Christ is the Head, and the church is His Body. Since the Head is an organism, the Body must also be an organism. Hence, organization has no place in the church.

Some may ask, "Since there are elders in the church, is this not an organization?" Apparently it seems to be an organization, but actually the eldership is not an organization. The elders are such not by their position but by their degree of life in the Lord. This is why 1 Peter 5 charges the elders to shepherd the flock of God among them, not lording it over them but becoming examples to the flock (vv. 1-3). This shows us that in the church the elders are there not by organization but by their life; they are to be the examples to the flock. A sheep is a very communal animal; the whole flock follows the leading of one head sheep. The elders are the head sheep. On the one hand, the elders are like the shepherds. But actually, the Lord did not ask them to be the shepherds. Rather, He charged them to be the head sheep, taking the lead in everything. Hence, this is not organizational but organic. It is not based on arrangement but on life. For example, while I am speaking here, not only does my mouth move, my whole being—hands, head, eyes, feet, and the whole body—move as well. When one part of the body is sick, the whole body cares for it. This is not by arrangement nor is it artificial. Rather, it is something organic.

Some have said that the local church is an autonomous congregation: each should be governed by itself, and all the localities are separate. Seemingly this saying is correct. Actually it is wrong because each church is not an individual body. The Body is the sum total of all the churches added together. In a body one cannot carve out any autonomy. If the shoulder, the arm, the hands, the head, the chest, and the legs all separate themselves into autonomies, the body is completely dismembered. Even though superficially we may distinguish the different parts of the body, the blood circulation within them cannot be separated. Two weeks ago we were visiting an elderly sister just as a middle-aged sister came to treat this one's leg pain with acupuncture. It was so wonderful that by putting the needle in the sister's finger, the pain in her leg was gone. This tells us that the human body is organic and is an integrated whole. Also, 1 Corinthians 12:26 says that when one member suffers, all the members suffer with it. Hence, a body cannot be divided, and none of its members can be independent and autonomous.

When we say that the church is organic, we do not mean that it is an organism composed of our natural life. Rather, it is an organism composed of the life in our spirit, which is Christ Himself. The resurrected Christ is the life-giving Spirit. This Spirit enters into us who have received Him. Hence, within us we have the same life and the same spirit. In this one life we become organic, being joined together as one. The problem now is that we have two lives within us. One is the original natural life; the other is the Lord Jesus as our life. Which life are we living by? If we live by our natural life, we are not the church. If we live according to Christ and live Christ, we are the church. The church is Christ Himself in all of us. When Christ is in Himself, He is just Christ. When He enters into the saints and lives with the saints, the Christ within the saints becomes the church. The reality of the church is Christ living in us. The key to the building up of the Body of Christ is to live Christ. If we live our natural life, the Body of Christ will not be built up. For this reason we must deny and reject our natural life and must put the natural life aside. In this way, Christ will have the proper place within us and will be able to increase day by day. This is the building up of the Body of Christ. The Body of Christ grows by the growth of Christ within us and is built up this way.

THE PERFECTED SAINTS DIRECTLY BUILDING UP THE BODY OF CHRIST

In the last chapter we have seen that in the building up of the Body of Christ the first One who builds is Christ. How does Christ build the church? He does it in His ascended position by giving to the church gifts such as the apostles, the prophets, the evangelists, and the shepherds and teachers. The Lord does not build up the church directly. Rather, it is the gifts given to the church that perfect the saints. The perfected saints in turn participate in the work of the ministry to directly build up the Body of Christ. Here is the distinction between the church in the Lord's recovery and the denominations. The denominations are built up as a congregation by a few pastors and preachers. But the church in the Lord's recovery is built up as the Body of Christ by every perfected saint.

Holding to Truth in Love

Ephesians 4:15 shows us that to build up the Body of Christ we first need to hold to truth in love. In the universe everything is vain and empty; there is no truth. According to Ephesians, in the universe there are only three things that are true and will last to eternity. The first is God's New Testament economy. This is very practical and real. We have to hold to this in love. This love is not our own love; rather, it is the love of God in Christ becoming our love. By this love we love God, Christ, and the church. We have to hold to God's economy in this love. The second thing is the all-inclusive Christ. Christ is most real. All other doctrines, speakings, and different teachings are not real. We must hold to Christ and forsake everything else. The third thing is the church as Christ's Body, the organism. The church is also true and will last for eternity because it is the Body of Christ, the true One. To build up the Body of Christ we must hold to these three things. All the other things we must reject.

Growing into Christ the Head in All Things

In order to build up the Body of Christ, we also need to grow up into Christ the Head in all things (Eph. 4:15). Although we are saved, in many things we are still outside of Christ. We need to grow into Christ in one thing after another. For example, when the sisters are going to make a dress, they often make their own decisions in choosing the style, the color, and the fabric. They do not allow the Lord to be Lord. Likewise, the brothers may not allow the Lord to be Lord in deciding whether they should leave their hair long or short. In too many things we have not allowed Christ to be Lord. Hence, in those things we are not in the Lord but rather outside the Lord. For this reason we need to grow. We need to grow into the Lord in one thing after another. This requires that we acknowledge the headship of Christ. When a sister is going to make a dress, she should pray to the Lord, "Lord, I am not the Lord. You are the Lord. You decide what style, color, and fabric the dress should be." In this way, she will grow into Christ. Second, we have to let Christ increase and grow in all of our inward parts. When Christ grows within us, we will grow in Him. Actually, the growth in life is not our growth, but the growth of the Lord Jesus in us. This requires that we give Him the ground and acknowledge His headship. We have to hand over our rights to Him and allow Him to have the ground in us. In this way, He will occupy us and will grow in us, and we will grow in His life. By this, we will grow into Christ the Head in all things.

Out from the Head

Our growth in life is a growth into Christ the Head. But our function in the Body of Christ is a function out from the Head. First we grow into the Head. Then out from the Head

THE BUILDING UP OF THE BODY OF CHRIST

and based upon the Head, we have something for the building up of His Body.

All the Body Causing the Growth of the Body of Christ

When we all allow Christ to grow within us, the result will be that all of us cause the growth of the Body of Christ. Ephesians 4:16 shows us that letting Christ grow within us unto the growth of the Body of Christ is first through every joint of the rich supply. These joints are the gifts mentioned in verse 11. They are the specially gifted members of the Body of Christ, and they are there for the supply of every member of the Body of Christ. Second, it is through the operation in measure of each one part, which is each of the members of the Body of Christ. When all the saints, who are the members of the Body of Christ, are supplied and perfected, they will all function according to their measure. This causes the growth, which is the building up, of the Body of Christ.

All the Body Being Built Together

When all the joints of the Body are supplying, and when each of the members of the Body is functioning, the Body is one. This oneness is the building. The building up of the whole Body is, on the one hand, through the fitting together, and on the other hand, through the knitting together. To be fitted together is for all the frame of the Body to be fitted together to form one structure. This is like the human body with its skeleton. In the skeleton there are the joints which fit the bones together to form one system. To be knitted together is for all the other parts to be joined to the skeleton and to be knit together into one Body. This is also like building a house. First, we join the whole frame together. Next, we fill up all the holes in the frame part by part. In this way the whole building is built up together through the fitting and the knitting. Thus, the whole Body becomes one. Here there are no human opinions or ideas; there is only the operation of the Spirit and the living of Christ within us. The result is that the Body builds itself up.

The Body Building Itself Up

Ephesians 4:16 shows us that when the Body of Christ is fitted and knit together, the Body is built up by itself (Eph. 4:16b). This building is in love, which means in the element and sphere of the divine love. This kind of building is also the direct building of the Body of Christ by the members of the Body of Christ. It is difficult to find such a situation in Christianity today. I hope that in the Lord's recovery our co-workers and the gifted ones would not only do the building work themselves, but would also perfect the saints, that the saints would function one by one and would directly build up the Body of Christ. May God bless us all that we would all see this vision of the building up of the Body of Christ.

A message given by Brother Witness Lee in Seoul, Korea on November 8, 1988.

About the Author

Witness Lee was born in 1905 in northern China and raised in a Christian family. At age 19 he was fully captured for Christ and immediately consecrated himself to preach the gospel for the rest of his life. Early in his service, he met Watchman Nee, a renowned preacher, teacher, and writer. Witness Lee labored together with Watchman Nee under his direction. In 1934 Watchman Nee entrusted Witness Lee with the responsibility for his publication operation, called the Shanghai Gospel Bookroom.

Prior to the Communist takeover in 1949, Witness Lee was sent by Watchman Nee and his other co-workers to Taiwan to ensure that the things delivered to them by the Lord would not be lost. Watchman Nee instructed Witness Lee to continue the former's publishing operation abroad as the Taiwan Gospel Bookroom, which has been publicly recognized as the publisher of Watchman Nee's works outside China. Witness Lee's work in Taiwan manifested the Lord's abundant blessing. From a mere 350 believers, newly fled from the mainland, the churches in Taiwan grew to 20,000 in five years.

In 1962 Witness Lee felt led of the Lord to come to the United States, settling in California. During his 35 years of service in the U.S., he ministered in weekly meetings and weekend conferences, delivering several thousand spoken messages. Much of his speaking has since been published as over 400 titles. Many of these have been translated into over fourteen languages. He gave his last public conference in February 1997 at the age of 91.

He leaves behind a prolific presentation of the truth in the Bible. His major work, *Life-study of the Bible,* comprises over 25,000 pages of commentary on every book of the Bible from the perspective of the believers' enjoyment and experience of God's divine life in Christ through the Holy Spirit. Witness Lee was the chief editor of a new translation of the New Testament into Chinese called the Recovery Version and directed the translation of the same into English. The Recovery Version also appears in a number of other languages. He provided an extensive body of footnotes, outlines, and spiritual cross references. A radio broadcast of his messages can be heard on Christian radio stations in the United States. In 1965 Witness Lee founded Living Stream Ministry, a non-profit corporation, located in Anaheim, California, which officially presents his and Watchman Nee's ministry.

Witness Lee's ministry emphasizes the experience of Christ as life and the practical oneness of the believers as the Body of Christ. Stressing the importance of attending to both these matters, he led the churches under his care to grow in Christian life and function. He was unbending in his conviction that God's goal is not narrow sectarianism but the Body of Christ. In time, believers began to meet simply as the church in their localities in response to this conviction. In recent years a number of new churches have been raised up in Russia and in many eastern European countries.

Other Books Published By
Living Stream Ministry

Titles by Witness Lee:

Abraham—Called by God	978-0-7363-0359-0
The Experience of Life	978-0-87083-417-2
The Knowledge of Life	978-0-87083-419-6
The Tree of Life	978-0-87083-300-7
The Economy of God	978-0-87083-415-8
The Divine Economy	978-0-87083-268-0
God's New Testament Economy	978-0-87083-199-7
The World Situation and God's Move	978-0-87083-092-1
Christ vs. Religion	978-0-87083-010-5
The All-inclusive Christ	978-0-87083-020-4
Gospel Outlines	978-0-87083-039-6
Character	978-0-87083-322-9
The Secret of Experiencing Christ	978-0-87083-227-7
The Life and Way for the Practice of the Church Life	978-0-87083-785-2
The Basic Revelation in the Holy Scriptures	978-0-87083-105-8
The Crucial Revelation of Life in the Scriptures	978-0-87083-372-4
The Spirit with Our Spirit	978-0-87083-798-2
Christ as the Reality	978-0-87083-047-1
The Central Line of the Divine Revelation	978-0-87083-960-3
The Full Knowledge of the Word of God	978-0-87083-289-5
Watchman Nee—A Seer of the Divine Revelation ...	978-0-87083-625-1

Titles by Watchman Nee:

How to Study the Bible	978-0-7363-0407-8
God's Overcomers	978-0-7363-0433-7
The New Covenant	978-0-7363-0088-9
The Spiritual Man • 3 volumes	978-0-7363-0269-2
Authority and Submission	978-0-7363-0185-5
The Overcoming Life	978-1-57593-817-2
The Glorious Church	978-0-87083-745-6
The Prayer Ministry of the Church	978-0-87083-860-6
The Breaking of the Outer Man and the Release ...	978-1-57593-955-1
The Mystery of Christ	978-1-57593-954-4
The God of Abraham, Isaac, and Jacob	978-0-87083-932-0
The Song of Songs	978-0-87083-872-9
The Gospel of God • 2 volumes	978-1-57593-953-7
The Normal Christian Church Life	978-0-87083-027-3
The Character of the Lord's Worker	978-1-57593-322-1
The Normal Christian Faith	978-0-87083-748-7
Watchman Nee's Testimony	978-0-87083-051-8

Available at
Christian bookstores, or contact Living Stream Ministry
2431 W. La Palma Ave. • Anaheim, CA 92801
1-800-549-5164 • www.livingstream.com